Health Care: Conditions and Needs of People 75 Years Old and Older: HRD-80-7

U.S. Government Accountability Office (GAO)

The BiblioGov Project is an effort to expand awareness of the public documents and records of the U.S. Government via print publications. In broadening the public understanding of government and its work, an enlightened democracy can grow and prosper. Ranging from historic Congressional Bills to the most recent Budget of the United States Government, the BiblioGov Project spans a wealth of government information. These works are now made available through an environmentally friendly, print-on-demand basis, using only what is necessary to meet the required demands of an interested public. We invite you to learn of the records of the U.S. Government, heightening the knowledge and debate that can lead from such publications.

Included are the following Collections:

Budget of The United States Government
Presidential Documents
United States Code
Education Reports from ERIC
GAO Reports
History of Bills
House Rules and Manual
Public and Private Laws

Code of Federal Regulations
Congressional Documents
Economic Indicators
Federal Register
Government Manuals
House Journal
Privacy act Issuances
Statutes at Large

COMPTROLLER GENERAL OF THE UNITED STATES
WASHINGTON, D.C. 20548

OCTOBER 15, 1979

B-165430

The Honorable Mario Biaggi
Chairman, Subcommittee on
   Human Services
House Select Committee on Aging

110594

Dear Mr. Chairman:

   Subject: Conditions and Needs of People 75 Years Old
            and Older (HRD-80-7)

      Pursuant to your March 14, 1979, letter and subsequent
discussions held with your office, we have included in two
enclosures to this letter information on the well-being of
people 75 years old and older, their need for services, and
the cost of providing services to these people. As agreed
with your office, we have presented the information you
requested in a question and answer format.

      The information contained in the enclosures is based on
our study of the personal conditions of older people in
Cleveland, Ohio. Three other reports have been issued on
this study entitled (1) "The Well-Being of Older People in
Cleveland, Ohio" (HRD-77-70, Apr. 19, 1977), (2) "Conditions
of Older People: National Information System Needed"
(HRD-79-95, Sept. 20, 1979), and (3) "Home Health--The Need
for a National Policy to Better Provide for the Elderly"
(HRD-78-19, Dec. 30, 1977).

      We could not obtain national estimates of the cost of
help provided to people 75 years old and older from all
sources. The results of our work are not statistically
projectable to the entire Nation. However, because your
office said that projections based on the Cleveland results
would be beneficial and helpful to the Subcommittee and your
office requested us to do so, we have projected the results
of our studies in Cleveland, Ohio, to the estimated 7.8 million noninstitutionalized people 75 years old and older in
1975 in the Nation. We emphasize that the estimates presented were not made on a statistical basis.

007364   (104037)

In summary, our review shows that

--people 75 years old and older are generally in a worse condition than those 65 to 74 years old;

--the greatest unmet needs for people 75 years old and older were for financial, social-recreational, and developmental services;

--overall, 61 percent of the people 75 years old and older needed help, in addition to that which they were already receiving;

--in fiscal year 1976, the average annual cost of providing help to each person 75 years old and older was $7,413--$4,682 received from agencies and the remaining $2,731 from family and friends;

--expansion of the six kinds of help we identified to all people 75 years old and older who need it would mean a 24-percent increase in this cost for the first year;

--the costs to expand help to all people 75 years old and older could be reduced considerably in the long run because expanded help leads to better conditions and less need for help in the future; and

--about 11 percent of the people 65 years old and older who are in institutions have conditions that indicate they could be maintained outside an institution in a congregate living environment. (For a definition of congregate living environment, see p. 10 of enc. I.)

As requested by your office, we did not obtain comments from the Department of Health, Education, and Welfare.

B-165430

    As arranged with your office, we will send copies of
this report to the Secretary of Health, Education, and
Welfare and to the Commissioner of Aging and make copies
available to others upon request.

                        Sincerely yours,

                        Comptroller General
                        of the United States

Enclosures - 2

QUESTIONS AND ANSWERS ABOUT

PEOPLE 75 YEARS OLD AND OLDER

The purpose of our Cleveland, Ohio, study was to assist the Congress and the executive branch in planning and dealing with various issues affecting older people by demonstrating what can be learned by assessing the well-being of older people and how these people are affected by the many services designed to aid them. Information from this study was used in preparing this report. The results of our work are not statistically projectable to the entire Nation. However, as requested, we have made national estimates based on the Cleveland results.

Cleveland, was selected for the study because of the community's willingness to participate. Over 100 agencies provided us with service information on older people. The Cleveland Foundation was particularly helpful to us in arranging for interviews and acting as a catalyst in obtaining the support of Cleveland agencies.

We took a sample from over 80,000 older people in the city who were 65 years old and older and who were not in institutions, such as nursing homes. In our study, 1,609 people were interviewed for us by Case Western Reserve University personnel from June through November 1975. A year later, 1,311 of these people were reinterviewed.

About 41 percent (544 of 1,311) of our sample of older people in Cleveland, were 75 years old or older. We used this group of older people to perform the following analyses. When comparisons were required, the people 75 years old and older were compared to the remainder of the sample who were 65 to 74 years old. Our responses to your questions follow.

1. Question: How do the personal conditions--health, security, loneliness, outlook on life--of people 75 years old and older compare to the personal conditions of people 65 to 74 years old? What percentage of the 65 to 74 year old group are functionally impaired; that is, people who are unable to do one or more daily tasks even if helped?

   Answer: For this analysis we used the results of the interviews obtained in 1975 to define and measure four personal conditions--health, security, loneliness, outlook on life--and divided the interviews into two groups. The first group was composed of people 65 to 74 years

old and the second of people 75 years old and older. A
comparison of the personal conditions of these two groups
showed that people 75 years old and older were generally
in a worse condition than those 65 to 74 years old. A
comparison of the personal conditions of the two age
groups as we defined them is shown in the following two
tables. The first table shows the personal conditions
of people 65 to 74 years old.

Conditions (note a)	Level of conditions			
	Best	Marginal	Worst	Total
	——(percent of sample)——			
Health	61	25	14	100
Security	b/51	b/25	b/24	100
Loneliness	64	25	11	100
Outlook on life	28	49	23	100
Overall	35	47	18	100

The personal conditions of people 75 years old and older
are shown in the following table.

Conditions (note a)	Level of conditions			
	Best	Marginal	Worst	Total
	——(percent of sample)——			
Health	42	32	26	100
Security	b/52	b/24	b/24	100
Loneliness	55	31	14	100
Outlook on life	20	51	29	100
Overall	26	49	25	100

a/For a description of conditions and level of conditions,
   see the methodology in enclosure II.

b/No statistically significant difference between the age
   groups shown in the two tables at this level of personal
   condition.

Only 8 percent of the people who are 65 to 74 years old
are functionally impaired as compared to 18 percent of the
people 75 years old and older. We defined functional impairment in terms of a person's ability to perform daily tasks.
Daily tasks include preparing meals, bathing, walking,
shopping, and eating. If an older person could not do one
or more of these tasks even if helped, he/she was considered
functionally impaired. The following two tables show the
ability to do daily tasks for people in the 65 to 74 years
old and the 75 year old and older age groups.

Estimate of the Percentage of People Who Are Functionally Impaired by Age Group

People 65 to 74 years old

Ability to do daily tasks	Percent of people in sample	Projection of number of people nationwide (note a) (millions)
Able to do all tasks without help	71	9.4
Can do all daily tasks but only with help in one or more	21	2.8
Cannot do one or more tasks even with help	8	1.0
Total	100	13.2

a/Projection based on an estimated 13.2 million people 65 to
  74 years old in 1975.

3

People 75 years old and older

Ability to do daily tasks	Percent of people in sample	Projection of number of people nationwide (note a)
		(millions)
Able to do all tasks without help	46	3.6
Can do all daily tasks but only with help in one or more	36	2.8
Cannot do one or more tasks even with help	18	1.4
Total	100	7.8

a/Projection based on an estimated 7.8 million people 75 years old and older in 1975.

2. Question: What percent of the people 75 years old and older (1) are not in need of services and (2) are in need of services? For those in need of services, what percent are not receiving all the help needed?

Answer: We determined the types of assistance needed by people 75 years old and older and compared their needs to the help they were receiving for six kinds of help. This comparison showed the extent of unmet needs by kinds of help. The kinds of help that were reaching the least proportion of those in need were financial, social-recreational, and developmental. Overall, 73 percent of these people needed some kind of help—12 percent received all the help needed and 61 percent needed additional help. The following table shows the unmet needs of people 75 years old and older for each kind of help.

4

Kind of help	Definition of need	Percent of sample not in need	In need	Percent of sample	
				Receiving all the help needed	Not receiving all the help needed
Medical treatment	Have illness that interferes a great deal with activities	61	39	16	23
Compensatory	Cannot do daily task without help	46	54	35	19
Financial	Inadequacy in amount of money	84	16	-	16
Social-recreational	Infrequent social contacts	81	19	1	18
Caregiving	No one available to help if older person becomes sick or disabled or help available only now and then	86	14	5	9
Developmental	Negative outlook on life	71	29	1	28
Overall	One or more of the above	27	73	12	61

3. Question: What is the current cost of services by source (family and friends and agencies) for people 75 years old and older? If these costs were projected nationally, what would the costs be for all people 75 years old and older?

Answer: We could not obtain national estimates of the cost of help provided to older people from all sources. The results of our work are not statistically projectable to the entire Nation. However, as requested, we have made national estimates based on the Cleveland results for the estimated 7.8 million noninstitutionalized older people 75 years old and older in 1975 in the Nation. These projections show that about $58 billion in help is provided annually to the 7.8 million people in this country who are 75 years old and older and live outside institutions. About 63 percent of the help older people receive is provided through Federal, State, local, and private agencies. Most of this help is federally funded.

5

In Cleveland the annual cost of providing these kinds of help to people 75 years old and older averaged $7,413 per person in fiscal year 1976. Various agencies provided $4,682 worth of help, and family and friends provided the remaining $2,731, as shown in the following table.

Average Annual Cost of Help for Each Person in Cleveland 75 Years Old and Older

Kind of help	From family and friends	From agencies	Total Dollars	Total Percent	Our projected national estimate (note a)
					(billions)
Medical treatment	$ —	$1,039	$1,039	14.02	$ 8.10
Compensatory	2,492	740	3,232	43.60	25.20
Financial	237	2,768	3,005	40.54	23.50
Social-recreational (note b)	—	130	130	1.75	1.00
Caregiving	2	4	6	.08	.05
Developmental (note b)	—	1	1	.01	.01
	$2,731	$4,682	$7,413	100.0	$57.9
Percent	37	63	100		

a/Projected national estimate based on the total cost of services from all sources and an estimated 7.8 million people 75 years old and older in 1975 who are not institutionalized. These projections are for illustrative purposes only.

b/As defined in our review, these kinds of help can only be provided by agencies.

As shown, the greatest portion (44 percent) of the cost
of help is for compensatary help, followed by financial help
(41 percent), and medical help (14 percent). Social-
recreational help accounts for only 2 percent, and caregiving and developmental help each account for less than
1 percent.

Comparing sources of help, the families and friends 1/
of older people provide 77 percent ($2,492 of $3,232) of the
compensatory help by performing daily tasks for them, and
only about 8 percent of the financial help ($237 of $3,005).
The other kinds are provided mostly by public and private
agencies funded under Federal programs. From the agencies'
standpoint, 59 percent of their cost was in financial help
($2,768 of $4,682) and 22 percent in treatment of illnesses
($1,039 of $4,682).

4.   Question: What would be the first year and long range
      cost to expand help to all people 75 years old and older
      who are in need? What would be the national costs of
      expanded help if projected to the entire population
      75 years old and older?

      Answer: It should be recognized that our national
      estimates are not statistically projectable.

Expansion of all six kinds of help to all people 75 years
old and older who need the help would mean a 24-percent increase ($1,770) in per person cost for the first year.
Nationally, this would mean a $13.8 billion increase. More
than half ($8 billion) of this additional cost to expand
help would be for financial help.

Nearly one-third ($4.2 billion) would be needed for
compensatory help and about $1 billion would go for medical
help. The following table shows the average costs per person along with our estimates of cost to expand each kind
of help to those in need. These estimates do not reflect
added costs due to the predicted increase in the older
population in the future or to inflation.

1/For a description of the method of costing family and friend
    services, see page 12.

Kind of help	Average cost per person without expand-ing help	Estimated first-year costs to expand help to people 75 years old and older		Percent of total additional cost
		Average per person	National total estimate	
		(millions)		
Medical treat-ment	$1,039	$ 132	$ 1,031	7.5
Compensa-tory	3,232	537	4,193	30.3
Financial	3,005	1,029	8,034	58.1
Social-recrea-tional	130	64	500	3.6
Caregiving	6	2	16	.1
Develop-mental	1	6	47	.4
Total	$7,413	$1,770	$13,821	100.0
Percent increase		24		

If the family and friends of older people do not absorb any of the $13.8 billion increase, public costs would have to increase by more than one-third (38 percent) to expand help to all those in need. However, if the family and friends could be encouraged to provide more compensatory help (in the same proportion as they did in 1975), public costs would have to be increased by much less. Nationally, we estimate that $3.2 billion less ($10.6 billion) public money would be required to expand help if family and friends would provide this additional compensatory help.

Based on our estimates, the projected first-year costs to provide expanded medical and compensatory help ($5.2 billion) could be totally offset by a reduction in medical help in future years because of improved medical conditions of older people receiving the expanded care.

5. Question: What percentage of the people 65 years old
    and older who are currently in institutions might be
    maintained outside these institutions?

    Answer: We estimate that about 11 percent of people
    65 years old and older in Cleveland who are in institu-
    tions could be maintained outside an institution in a
    congregate living environment.

    In our report entitled "Home Health--The Need for a
National Policy to Better Provide for the Elderly" (HRD-78-19,
Dec. 30, 1977), we noted that older people in institutions
are more impaired than those not in institutions. For example, 87 percent of the institutionalized people are greatly
or extremely impaired while only 14 percent of the noninstitutionalized have the same impairment levels.

    Of the 13 percent in institutions who were not greatly
or extremely impaired, some had impairments which might
require services other than those usually provided in congregate housing. The remaining older people--about 11 per-
cent--were mildly or moderately impaired in activities of
daily living and were no worse than moderately impaired in
physical condition. These people could use congregate housing. In Cleveland we estimated 356 of 3,295 nursing home
residents could use congregate housing.

    The average annual cost of maintaining these 356 people
in Cleveland in institutions was $2.0 million compared to
$1.5 million in congregate housing, and $1.8 million in the
community. About $0.5 million less would be required annually
to maintain these people in congregate housing than in institutions, as shown in the following table.

| Location | Average cost per person | | Annual cost for 356 people | |
	Daily	Annually	Total	Difference from institution
				(millions)
Institution	$15.27	$5,574	$2.0	$ -
Congregate housing	11.32	3,134	1.5	0.5
Community	13.95	5,023	1.8	0.2

Community costs were based on average agency and family and friend service costs in Cleveland in the period October 1976 to March 1977 for older people who could use congregate housing. Congregate housing costs were 1974-75 costs adjusted for inflation to 1977 costs and were obtained from a Department of Housing and Urban Development study of 27 congregate housing and Urban Development study of 27 congregate housing sites. For this study, congregate housing was defined as housing where eight main services are provided, namely: meals, social-recreational, education, transportation, medical care, home-maker, counseling, and security. Institutional costs were based on January to February 1977 Medicaid costs for skilled nursing and intermediate care in Ohio facilities.

METHODOLOGY

The information contained in this report is based on our study of the personal conditions of older people in Cleveland, Ohio. Three other reports have been issued on this study entitled (1) "The Well-Being of Older People in Cleveland, Ohio" (HRD-77-70, Apr. 19, 1977), (2) "Conditions of Older People: National Information System Needed" (HRD-79-95, Sept. 20, 1979), and (3) "Home Health--The Need for a National Policy to Better Provide for the Elderly" (HRD-78-19, Dec. 30, 1977). Following are the details of the data gathering and analytical methodology from the two-phase study.

WELL-BEING STATUS AND SERVICES DATA BASES

We took a sample from over 80,000 people in Cleveland, Ohio, who were 65 years old and older and were not in institutions, such as nursing homes. We insured that our sample was demographically representative by comparing the characteristics of our sample to statistics for the city of Cleveland.

In our study, 1,609 older people were interviewed by Case Western Reserve University personnel from June through November 1975. A year later, 1,311 of these older people were reinterviewed.

In interviewing, we used a questionnaire containing 101 questions developed by a multidisciplinary team at the Duke University Center, in collaboration with HEW's Administration on Aging, former Social and Rehabilitation Service, and Health Resources Administration. The questionnaire contains questions about an older person's well-being status in five areas of functioning--social, economic, mental, physical, and activities of daily living.

To identify factors that could affect the well-being of older people, we

--developed specific definitions of services being provided to older people and dimensions for quantifying the services;

--identified the providers of the services--families and friends, health care providers, and over 100 social service agencies;

--obtained information about the services provided to each person in our sample and the source and intensity of these services; and

--developed an average unit cost for each of the 28 services.

In defining and quantifying the services, we used a format developed by the Duke University Center to define 28 different services. These services are defined in appendix V of our prior report. 1/ Services are defined according to four elements: purpose, activity, relevant personnel, and unit of measure. For example, meal preparation was defined as follows:

Purpose: To regularly prepare meals for an
              individual.

Activity: Meal planning, food preparation, and
              cooking.

Relevant
  personnel: Cook, homemaker, family member.

Unit of
  measure: Meals.

Examples: Meals provided under 42 U.S.C. 3045
              (supp. V, 1975), the Older Americans Act,
              and meals-on-wheels programs.

To quantify the service, we used the unit of measure along with the duration, or number of months, during which the service was received.

We also developed an average unit cost for each service based on the experience of 27 Federal, State, local, and private agencies in Cleveland between October 1976 and March 1977. We compared these costs to similar costs in Chicago, Illinois, and Durham, North Carolina. As discussed in our prior report, the family and friends are also important sources of services. In their absence, any services received would have to be from an agency. Therefore, we assigned the same cost to family and friend services that we found for agencies.

1/"The Well-Being of Older People in Cleveland, Ohio,"
   Apr. 19, 1977, HRD-77-70.

Each piece of data was collected so that it could be related to an individual in our sample. This included the questionnaire data, data on the 28 services provided by social service agencies, and data on the services provided by health care providers. By relating these data to the individual, we were able to do comparative analyses of sampled older people for over 500 different variables.

ANALYTICAL TECHNIQUES

In our prior report, we combined the five areas of functioning—(1) social, (2) economic, (3) mental, (4) physical, and (5) activities of daily living—into a well-being status because we wanted to consider the entire person. We described well-being status as (1) unimpaired, (2) slightly impaired, (3) mildly impaired, (4) moderately impaired, (5) generally impaired, (6) greatly impaired, (7) very greatly impaired, or (8) extremely impaired.

The Duke University Center's questionnaire is unique in that data from the questionnaire can be aggregated into a number of useful measures, each with a specific purpose. As previously discussed, the questionnaire can provide a five-dimensional functional assessment or be combined into a well-being status that we used in our first report. This assessment was not designed, however, for determining the benefits of help for older people. Through our analyses, we were able to develop useful measures of personal conditions of, problems of, and help available to older people. The conditions of older people used in this report—health, security, loneliness, and outlook on life—are described on the following page.

Health condition

An older person's health condition is the ability to do daily tasks. In categorizing a person's ability to do daily tasks, we considered his or her responses to questions on 13 different tasks. For example, regarding meal preparation, each person was asked "Can you prepare your own meals * * * without help, with some help, or are you completely unable to prepare any meals?" We then categorized each person based on the number of the 13 tasks they needed some help with or were completely unable to do. For most of this report we used three categories—(1) can do all 13 tasks without help, (2) need help with one or more but can do all with help, and (3) cannot do any even with help.

13

CONDITIONS

Level of condition	Illness	Health Ability to do daily tasks (note a)	Overall	Security	Loneliness	Outlook on life	Overall personal condition
Best	No illness that interferes a great deal with activities	Can do all 13 daily tasks without help	In best category for both illness condition and ability to do daily tasks	Worries hardly ever	Feels lonely almost never	Does not feel useless and finds life exciting	(1) In best category for all 4 conditions or (2) Best for 3 and marginal for the other
Marginal	One illness that interferes a great deal with activities	Can do all 13 daily tasks but only with help in one or more	(1) In best category for illness condition or ability to do daily tasks and marginal in other or (2) in marginal category for both	Worries fairly often	Feels lonely sometimes	(1) Finds life exciting but feels useless or (2) Does not feel useless but finds life dull or routine	(1) In marginal category for 2 or more conditions and best for other(s) or (2) In worst category for only one condition
Worst	Two or more illnesses that interfere a great deal with activities	Can't do at least one task even with help	In worst category for either illness condition or ability to do daily tasks	Worries very often	Feels lonely quite often	Feels useless and finds life routine or dull	In worst category for 2 or more conditions

a/Daily tasks include preparing meals, bathing, walking, shopping, eating, etc. Details on these daily tasks are described on pages 57 to 59 of appendix IV of our Apr. 19, 1977, report, "Well-Being of Older People in Cleveland, Ohio" (HRD-77-70).

14

If an older person is not in the best health condition, illnesses were used in defining the person's problems. In categorizing an older person's illness situation, we considered whether an older person had any of 27 different illnesses, including mental illnesses, and how much the illness interfered with his or her activities. For example, each person was asked if he or she had heart trouble. If the person said "yes," he or she was then asked "how much does it interfere with your activities--not at all, a little (some), or a great deal?" We then categorized each person based on the number of illnesses that interfered with his or her activities a great deal. For most of this report we used three categories--(1) those with no illnesses bothering them a great deal, (2) those with one, and (3) those with two or more.

Security condition

A person's security condition can be described by how often a person worries. How often a person worries can be related to the amount of income and caregiving help a person receives. In developing a person's security condition, we used the following question in the questionnaire:

--"How often would you say you worry about things-- very often, fairly often, or hardly ever?"

In defining security problems, we used the following three questions. To define a money problem, we asked:

--"How well does the amount of money you have take care of your needs--very well, fairly well, or poorly?"

And these questions were used in defining caregiving problems:

--"Is there someone who would give you any help at all if you were sick or disabled? If 'yes,' * * *"

--"Is there someone who would take care of you as long as needed, or only a short time, or only someone who would help you now and then * * *?"

Loneliness condition

A person's loneliness condition was identified using the following question:

--"Do you find yourself feeling lonely quite often, sometimes, or almost never?"

The information for identifying loneliness problems was obtained from the following questions:

--"About how many times did you talk to someone-- friends, relatives, or others--on the telephone in the past week?"

--"How many times during the past week did you spend some time with someone who does not live with you * * * not at all, once, two to six times, once a day or more?"

Using these questions, the following table shows infor- mation combined to establish a loneliness problem variable called social contacts.

How often a week talks on telephone	How often a week visits with someone			
	Once a day or more	Two to six times	Once	Not at all
Once a day or more	High	High	Medium	Medium
Two to six times	High	Medium	Medium	Low
Once	Medium	Medium	Low	Low
Not at all	Medium	Low	Low	Low

Using high, medium, and low activity as a measure of intensity of social contacts, this variable was related to loneliness condition.

Outlook on life condition

The outlook on life condition is obtained by defining life view using information from the questions shown in the following table.

Life is generally	Feel useless at times	
	Yes	No
Exciting	Fair	Good
Pretty routine	Poor	Fair
Dull	Poor	Fair

Using this information, we were able to define three levels of outlook on life condition--good, fair, and poor.

Overall condition

Because a person is at all times in some overall condition which results from the integration of each of the four conditions, we constructed a composite condition of a person illustrated as follows.

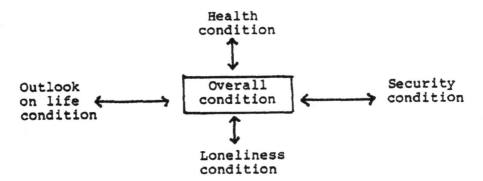

Our methodology and analytical results show that a useful measure of the conditions of a person can be developed. In some instances, such as the outlook on life condition, the amount of data for constructing this variable is minimal. Nevertheless, methodological concepts and analytical results show the existence of this condition. Further, our measures are logically equivalent to the five-dimensional functional assessment used in our prior report based on the Duke University Center's questionnaire. The health condition is equivalent to the mental, physical, and activities of daily living dimensions; the security condition is related to the economic dimension; and the loneliness condition is related to the social dimension.

Lightning Source UK Ltd.
Milton Keynes UK
UKOW04f0630130317
296494UK00009B/468/P